Micro Trading

How anyone can get into trading stocks, and beat the learning curve without losing Big on the way.

by

Sean Michael G.

https://www.facebook.com/Tordynamics

This book is a work of CreativeNon-fiction. Names, characters, places and incidents are either the product of the author's imagination or are used Creatively. Any resemblance to actual persons, living or dead, or to actual events or locales is entirely coincidental.

This ebook/ print book is licensed for your personal enjoyment only. This ebook may not be re-sold or given away to other people. If you like to share this book with another person, please purchase an additional copy for each person you share it with.

Copyright © 2018 Sean Michael G. All rights reserved. Including the right to reproduce this book or portions thereof, in any form. No part of this text may be reproduced in any form without the express written permission of the author. Microtrading is my own unique term to the style of trading taught herein, use of it in a for profit manner is forbidden, and purchase/ or viewing of this book is your agreement to that condition.

Version 2018.04.22

Author's Appreciation

I would like to start by giving thanks to my family, however strange, corrupted by wiles, and no matter how eccentric, thank you from the bottoms of my being to the upper echelons of my soul. Whether for good or for ill my life and mind were formed by your actions and words.

To my wonderful wife, a truly wonderful gift from God thank you for putting up with the weaker more troublesome half of our marriage. Marriage to you is certainly a pairing as we conquer each day together side by side. With you I can achieve more, accomplish more, and be more through and through. I love you Chon-Chon.

To my son, my son Wiyam you are a delight and a hellraiser. Your exuberance is a wonder to behold, even through most your life we had to be apart, you still loved me and didn't hold that against me. I love you son and I am proud of your scholastic achievements, as well as your extreme curiosity that reminds me the most of me at your age. Grow up I pray to be a man who loves God first then self, cherish people and their dreams, be a do-er not just for self, but to leave a legacy, an impact that betters the world long after your gone.

Thank you Editor, although that isn't your day job and you took long hours to fix the horror of my writing to help it achieve a readability I could never have hoped for without your efforts, although the bill seemed high, just kidding, thank you.

This might seem strange but thank you J-H, you were an influence that I have actually prayed wasn't ever in my life, but, it was that horror of your psyche that taught me to fear evil, you truly are the most evil person I have ever known. I do not regret saying it was the last time I let my hand down to try to raise you up, I am thankful you finally went so bad that it was a necessity to my own person-hood. I do pray you find good and walk away from evil, that is not to say to become perfect, just find God's grace and grow into a respectable man and father, before it is to late.

Test Students who allowed me to convince you to trust me to teach you a new skill I have created, to learn to Microtrade and be profitable. I had decided if I couldn't teach every one of you to be profitable I wouldn't pursue this style and teaching it to others, but you all accomplished so much, I'm flabbergasted. No words can say thank you enough, you share a place in my heart now, as family.

To the early readers who also had to try doing this scary new thing I created, and actually succeed at it so I could say my book was good and ready to go forward, thank you. I know you try thanking me now, but really it is you who walked out on that ledge with me and jumped. Thank you for being the great people that you are. You have taught me more than I taught you I think.

Finally to those in the future who take these words,

understanding the risk but stepping forward responsible for their own lives and make decisions to better their lives from the teachings garnered from this small book. Thank you for purchasing it, but if you stole it, I will forgive you, that is if you pay twice the price at minimum after your profits roll in. Please readers, it may seem like a repeating gif at times but please give great reviews and feedback as you make the leap and start making positive gains. It means a lot, I obviously do not teach this in hopes of amazing profits, I do it to solve a problem and help people not become a statistic. 90-95% of all traders end up losing it all. This was created in part to help those who don't want to be a loser, not become one. Yes it is simple and doesn't teach a million strategies, But it does teach you one that has always been in the market and is simple to follow. It gives you better odds, and reduces your risk. So as you go on to learn these skills remember me and post a good review, I thank you now for doing so.

About the Author

Hello folks, good to be here teaching you, well in the form of words captured and sent out I am here with you now. Some of you may know me, I am the eccentric man who likes to learn tons and tons of new skills and knowledge. My curiosity is ever an itch needing scratched. I went to school in a small town in Illinois, land of the biggest corruption of politicians, but also the land of Lincoln, a hero remembered even still. Lincoln is a good example as who remembers most of the presidents? Or how about who remembers half of them? Lincoln is so remembered not because of zombie killing as some movies have sensationalized, but because he changed the worlds fate, today America pushes for Liberty and freedom for all around the world, do you think that would have started if Lincoln hadn't made the biggest push here starting a landslide?

So me I want to be like that, I want to make a difference in the world. To make a lasting legacy. I want to build orphanages that are self sustaining, self supporting. It really isn't that hard to do. To make a single large investment that offers in perpetuity the funds and resources needed to feed clothe and raise children schooled for success emotionally and monetarily.

This dream isn't a reality without readers like you who buy the book and review me well. As I use funds from these side projects to get these projects undertaken and funded. So You are to thank for making it possible.

You probably know me now better than some hokey bio, you know where my heart and soul are, and what drives me. Each day I strive to become a better teacher and writer to make it easier and speedier to these goals. But an orphanage isn't my only dream, I dream of helping single mothers and fathers, the homeless and veterans. Those that need help I want to help. I look for new ways to learn to improve and to grow so that I can one day not be a blind man trying to lead the blind. No matter your station in life, you can always achieve more, but what will you be using it for?

Now my simple Bio: I'm near middle ages, fatter than I'd like to be, and college educated. I make enough to count me at upper middle class if not higher depending on who's definition you use. I have lived all over the world and all over my country. I speak English but sometimes pretend well that I can speak Espanol, Japanese, Chinese, German, and Illongo, and sometimes not so well, Romanian, Russian, and Marsian.

I'm Shorter than average but larger feet for my size. My head gets to big sometimes, but I will try to deflate every now and then. What are you doing reading this nonsense, skip to the important stuff.

Insider Reviews

Phil Star Investors Challenge *"This Book is not for the trader who has made it, this is the book for the trader that will make it...."*

Americana Stock trader Review *"Never did I think someone could reinvent a workable teaching method that reminded me of Jesse Livermores Bucket shop trading..."*

Editor @ Traders weekly *"This book didn't impress me until I asked my fourth grade son Travis to do a trade like what was described. I described how to do it and what to look for and my son 10 minutes later found a rebounder and made his lunch money for that day at school. Will be hoping for more like this..."*

Pawnshop Clerk Bill *"First time someone came in trying to give me something I didn't have to buy. I had often thought of trading especially after the Harvey show had Timothy Sykes on. Everything was always to scary and complicated, this was different, this book really is dumbed down and super stupid easy...."*

Martha Stuer *"Most of the book is unneeded for most, but that 10-20% is invaluable to most, Success has arrived"*

You Can Do It!

Table of Contents

<u>What is this</u>

<u>1-Before getting started</u>

<u>2- What is Microtrading</u>

<u>3-Reading Charts</u>

<u>4- Screeners/Scanners</u>

<u>5- Reading the Level2 Charts</u>

<u>6-Stocks in Play-End</u>

What is this?

You picked this book up, and you don't know that already? Good, that gives me hope you'll be a customer. Stock trading is a way to buy and sell partial to full ownership of publicly and privately held companies "shares". To be explained further inside.

Public companies trade openly on the public market. They are the ones I am talking about in this book. Private companies will not work. Think of it like this, public companies sell shares like flea markets or ebay sells products. Private companies trade like two buddies making a bet on a games outcome in the privacy of one of their own homes. One any one could attend within reason and buy or sell, and the other only a select few could have had the opportunity,

Before you go on reading, I will say I have taken some writing courses to improve my abilities from gutter trash to about the level of a recyclables heap. I appreciate the feedback even negative that keeps this in mind. Now I will not release a book again that is so poor as to be unreadable, or harmful to your sanity if you do. I have an editor to help with revisions and clean up. What you are buying in this book is a limited license to read and learn what is within this book. As the legalities stated, you don't own the words to use how you want to. So being so limited in purchase I do give content my fullest ambition, to make it so rich you can be satisfied even with a less then awesome writer teaching it to you.

So in this book I will show you how to micro trade stocks to limit risk while increasing rewards. Micro trading is actually more easily accomplished for a positive gain than standard trading such as daytrading or swing trading. In standard trading you need to not only make a profit, but make a profit that overcomes trading fees. These trading fees add up. They cause more hurt on a losing trade and less joy in earnings on a positive one.

Also trading fees limit foreigners who come from lower tier countries lacking financial resources to open accounts with large enough sums that the trades could offset trading fees. The average Joe or Jane may not feel comfortable with losing larger sums needed to trade to offset these fees either.. By being able to trade at the 5$-$50 range and make 5-20% a trade repeatably, even 2nd tier country citizenry could participate and make dramatic changes in their life. With incomes in countries such as the Philippines being in some areas 200-300 pesos a day or less, this equaling less than 4-6$ a day, making an extra two months of income a year would be a tremendous feat.

Oh hold on don't drop the book or close it and run off. Yes the trading level is micro, and yes the gains seem micro too.

BUT

Would you send your child to play baseball at 6 years old in the Majors try outs? Or would you rather send them to T-ball camp? T-ball camp it is and so is this. This is a wonderful way to get better at trading faster and learn without the big losses most have to endure to achieve it. Not only do a majority of traders lose all their money, but most lose it again and again. So for those with means to throw 50k in an account, even you will find much benefit to this teaching. Why take the costlier route of learning when with a little time and the same amount of patience you could achieve a better more productive route.

Deciding on the costlier route? That is NUTS! And, so you would be if your going to actually trade real dollars first. But you might say paper trading lets a person trade fake dollars. So many new traders are now taking advantage of this and trading artificially on real markets as practice. This however also has limits. Your not trading real money, your actions and feelings, even your executions etc will be different than a real trade.

So here in this book I'll teach you grade school trading tactics that let you learn real trading with only grade school consequences for when you foul, get a strike, get tackled or just plane run out of bounds etc, you wont be made destitute by the mistake, or made emotionally bankrupt.

1

Before getting started some of you need help on how to get started, such as getting a brokerage account where you can perform no cost trading, and how to get it funded. So how can you fund your account? With Robinhood they will give you a free stock when creating your account, and give you more stock when referring friends. That is at the time of this writing they are.

Now You know this and so I would appreciate the free stocks of any readers who open new accounts, by them following my link to open an account here.

https://share.robinhood.com/seang1165

By clicking that for your entry into Robinhood micro account trading your able to give me a tip for giving away this great info that can and will, if you allow it, change your life. Stock trading is liberating, and the building up of your account, slowly but surely is more fulfilling than the sledgehammer method of losing a small fortune just to learn approach is.

So now you have a link for an account setup, but how do you fund it? Well you will be given, if they are still offering it, a free stock share. That in of itself isn't much So your first step will be coming up with a plan of action. The plan of action will be your initial go to till your funded. In this plan of action you will address your dilemma and work towards a plausible solution to obtain a resolution favorable to your needs.

When funding your account being able to fund it with $200 or more dollars is great. Some however will not have that much to spare. Some others will think or believe they don't have what to spare at all, although they may think that they will be surprised of what can be accomplished with some creativity and good planning. So write down your basic financial status on a pad. Start with the plus's, these are your various income streams whether taxable or not.

In Example:

1. $1700.00 monthly income from full time job

2. $50.00 monthly income from mowing your neighbors' yard

Total= $1750

Now this is rough, a pretty bleak picture for say a single mother, or small family trying to make it living in the United States. Even still you would be surprised that with some creative budgeting, even in this situation, extra can in most cases be found, saved, and then implemented. Learning to take **YOUR** Life under control is important, probably the most important action you can take during your lifetime. An unplanned life isn't a life with no plan, it is a life with a plan to fail. Growing up isn't just getting older, it is maturing, learning that we do things not because we want to, but rather because we need to, or should, just so we could have a better outcome than if we did not.

It never ceases to amaze me how often people will tell me how this political leader, or that boss, or how it was all because of the color of their own skin, that they are in their shoes living where and how they live. I will listen to them politely, noticing an expensive phone that they have been using, maybe two young children by two different daddies, or designer jeans. I might glance out the window and see their car on $5,000 dollar wheels out of some rap video, or jewelry that could be sold at gold weight to pay a years worth of college. Very often these types of situations happen, but on occasion I will hear the person who just really doesn't have. The little they have so little they would be desperate to find a dollar extra. For the truly broke this next part is not for you. This again is not racial or cultural stereotyping, all cultures and races have those that fit the above examples. I myself contain near equal parts of all races and many cultural diversities in my upbringing.

    For those who blame others, life, situations etc, for your quality of life, WAKE UP! Your driving your life, not the president or senators, not centuries old history, not your country, not your momma. You have the steering wheel in your hands for your life. It is up to you if you'll keep driving down broken roads that waste your gas and leave you worn out. It is up to you to get a map out and take the time to plan a real proper route to take. So get the pencil or pen out and get your plan started, make your budget. Be realistic with your necessities and needs, and desires. If your in the lesser 20% on income levels should you be buying products in the highest 20-5% range? What I mean here is people with lower income shouldn't think it is a need to have products in the highest ranges price wise. If you're a twenty percenter from the bottom then buy a twenty percenter smart phone from the bottom, or a few year old better one that costs the same as the new one that's in that category. Buy name brand clothes, but from Flea Markets or Goodwill, or Just go to Walmart for new. Until you grow up and take control of your life, taking true responsibility you will be hard pressed to ever succeed. Wisdom in knowing your means and living at or below them.

So you got your incomes down on paper. Now jot down your monthly fixed expenses. These include your rent or mortgage. These fixed costs include utilities such as gas and electric. They also include food expenses. What they do not include are movie nights, cable, highspeed internet, and memberships to gyms etc. Your fixed expenses are the bills fixed that you need to pay to live and can not get them reduced reasonably. I may sound like a broken record but these are import details to find your success outside of fluke luck, like a winning lottery ticket.

1. Rent $675

2. Electric $125

3. Food(whats necessity not lobster tails or name brand cereals) $425

Now in this fixed expense include one more, it's a security expense, no not security like CCTV, but security as in I can pay my bills even I called in to work sick. This is 10% of whats left from fixed expenses being minus from the total income. This is your security fund, and should be allowed to grow untouched.

Now you have whats left to budget for your wants, and

desires etc. If you have $275 left your goal is to find slash your cravings to spend down so you can fund your account. If not you can keep spending it and staying in the life your in. This IS YOUR CHOICE. Cut those things down to $270 and you have found $60 a year to fund your account. Cut them down to $274 and you have $12.

Either one will work, but one is better for you long term, one is better for you short term. So make your plans, and every month go back over them and decide if you can do better or not. It may be that you start with a dollar a month and find three or four months later you can put another fifty bucks in this new Robinhood account you started.

So now you found the funds to fund your account, now all you need to do is get them from your bank account and into your trading account. The trading account is the Robinhood account you should have created earlier following this link. https://share.robinhood.com/seang1165 This is fairly simple just link your account at your bank using a debit card on Robinhoods website. They make it easy for you, then put in the amount you want to fund at that moment and transfer. Depending on the details you'll be able to trade in minutes or days but either way your account has been established.

Soon you'll be on tropical beaches like me sipping drinks and hearing the waves break. No actually you wont be unless your already able to do that. Trading right doesn't entail massive riches to magically appear in your portfolio. Trading is a job, takes time to learn it and get it, and monies wont teleport into your account, you'll have to work to get them in there. Don't get scared, hard work and learning can be rewarding and is satisfying.

Waking up each day plotting a basic sketch of what stocks you may trade and how, if the ifs happen, then following through with it is much more fulfilling then winning a scratch off. Watching your account go from $50 to $100 and on upwards to $1286 and up even still, is amazing. Inside your joy will overflow into other areas of your life. Making you a much more fulfilled existence.

I know others who just threw money at their trading accounts, no plans, no methods, just dreams. The ones still trading are really good at it, but most went broke before figuring out all the profit making moves.

Now I know others who barely funded an account and have made over $100,000 so far. The difference is this, learning it right or learning it till you get it right, or perfect practise makes perfect results. Learning something wrong just means much more effort in learning it right later, along with lots of lost time you will not get back.

So which do you wanna be? Now if you make six figures a year you may say, so what, and go about with your wallet like a sledgehammer. You can swing it around losing money with most of your trades until some system actually begins to look good. Then as your false confidence mounts you may go in deep on that sure thing, the system you found works and this is gravy. Next morning your brokerage is calling you, your short exploded over night when a billionaire announced his buy out plans on the company that had just announced fiscal troubles. You have lost over $50,000 in your big sledgehammer account, but also need to come up with $356,718 really fast. Why because shorting has infinite loss potential, no. Yes shorting does have infinite loss potential but that wasn't the cause, it was your overall strategy sucked and relied on luck to be on your side.

The bad about learning on your own, just hammering away isn't just the typical loses day after day. The bad is the false confidence of thinking you learned a system that works and losing everything or more than everything. No one should have to risk everything or more than they can afford in the stock market just for the prospect to make money.

The Stock market is one of the stablest investment platforms around, and in that only if you go about it with clear understanding. I have sat with those near tears who lost half their retirement during the 2008 Housing/ Banking crash. I asked if they read news reports talking about the bubble happening, these articles were everywhere for 2 plus years before the crash. All had heard, none reacted. If they had begun slowly moving into safeguard positions every single one of these folks would have made huge sums of money. One such Gentleman a teacher, now at a school they dread waking up and going to work to teach at lost more than a quarter million dollars, yet if they had implemented safeguards actively then repurchased those same stocks back after markets stabilized, that portfolio would be up over 350% at a bare minimum.

Don't set this book down just because you can afford a bigger account, this book is for every new trader. Every trader new to the craft or even not new but struggling still needs this book. This book as stated earlier teaches you the best approach to learning without high risk. Think about it logically for a minute. So you start with $300, and use this book to grow your account to $5,000, then in over confidence you finally have that big loss. You messed up and lost a third or more of it on a single or even a couple bad trades. So what! You are up! Why start high risking so much only to learn methods you probably shouldn't or are not ready for?

Learning to trade with less is easier and harder, easier in regards to you needing to evaluate trades with a more picky outlook. Making your gains start happening sooner than later due to a more practical outlook. Harder in that you have less options to choose from and it takes significantly longer to earn those nice big money paydays. It comes down to choice and wisdom, will you choose the wise approach or the fools highway.

2

So you kept up with it, you may have wisdom in you after all. In the previous chapter you learned how to get me and yourself a free stock, that is if they are still offering that perk at Robinhood. Some of you might not have been nice following my link to open your account. Your stingy and should make up for it by giving me a great 5 star review right now......yes now, go on. Thank you.

Ok I now either got a tip as a thank you through the starting of your account by following my link or hopefully a great review, thank you. I may not be much of a writer but I will teach you how to micro trade stocks for real gains. These skills are valuable and can change your life. That is if you take this book and your life seriously, you will see the value being built into it from here on out. They have already changed mine. Not many years ago I was just a fat truck driver. Injury and a desire to be more gave me the push to learn stock trading. Now don't think my only skill was being a trucker. I chose that because of the ease and pay. I could make near Doctor salaries by just working long hard hours and being away from a stable home life. After my injury in my search for learning I came across Timothy Sykes stuff and others. I even wrote a short book "Trucker to Trader" found on Amazon. That book showed how I journeyed from trucker to basic trader. It left out a lot of the stresses and trials I faced each day, but it wasn't ever meant to be exhaustive. This book is not exhaustive in its approach either, but it is really a great single source starter to get into trading with little money and learn faster and easier than other methods commonly used. This book will take you from no nothing, knowing nothing to funded account trading with a path to success easier and in a shorter lower stress time period.

You have so far in some few pages learned where to go to open an account and a basic idea on how to budget and save if need be to fund a new account for the first time. Now I hope you have done so already. There is no need to keep reading without having an account and having it funded. Sure you would still learn, but learning without doing is worthless. You would inevitably forget much of the details and may end up thinking in the future you still know enough of it to start trading only to find yourself making mistakes. Some may teach you knowledge gained has value but I'll tell you useless or knowledge you don't use, is worthless accept to hog valuable mental resources that better could be used elsewhere. Don't just day dream of trading stocks for profits and gains. Lets get out there and make it happen!

In stock trading you will find freedom, if you learn it right. This book will teach how I personally micro trade, to reduce risk and profit easier and more often than when trading the normal Daytraders approach. Everything in this book is but steps to growing and learning to trade better, and safer while you learn mastery over the general markets. Some will tell you this is flawed, because there can be no mastery over the general markets. I tell you they are flawed, every sector, every trade, every skill has a class of masters. Could you really call making in excess of a Billion USA dollars in the market less than being a master?

You to can join the ranks of master market traders even starting from such small accounts. In some regards you could be viewed masters once growing your accounts to 1000x your initial stakes and being right more than 90% of the time, with an average loss less than half average gains. Think now what it will feel like opening your app or web browser up and seeing your $100 account is now $100,000 and still growing well, trade after trade. At that point your investment in this book has paid out tremendously. I would bet you, if I was a gambling man, you will have read many more books like those in the back of this book in the recommended reading section, and even though you can now trade big bucks trades, you still micro trade when they are not available. See trading can have an addictive nature. This addictive nature blurs the vision of traders experienced and not and loses traders hard earned dollars. I found it in myself also, that is why I still micro trade even with the ability to trade bigger volume on bigger stocks. See micro trading allows you to trade more opportunities. Yes I said earlier the exact opposite about Micro Trading. I said that it is harder in that you need to be more picky. Both statements are true though. See Micro trading allows one to enter the market not down immediately due to trading fees or commissions. This once your account is far into the positive opens up more opportunities in what would be more speculative trading. Say a small rumor is barely out and not well heard around the traders corner. You could buy a few shares and if it pans out buy more into the gap up that will occur when news announcements confirm it, selling before the hype dies out. Yet, if on the other hand the news is just fluff you could easily bale on those few shares pulling out without even a loss if it hasn't moved down or up enough to cover the standard trading fees of other Brokerage accounts. One such opportunity is **Low Float** stocks. These stocks if one were to enter traditionally they would move the price dramatically, but to sell could cause just as much if not more dramatic of a swing. With these no cost trades you can enter in smaller volume orders over a period of time. No price fluctuating, and when the pumpers pump it your now good volume is ready for fast release, dumping the pumpers dreams down the drain where they belong.

In most cases you cannot trade these low float stocks without a greater risk or moving the market with just your own trade as discussed earlier. This is bordering on market manipulation even if unintended. This reminds me of Bill Bastour. He was a low float guy, he learned this gimmick trading method and made a lot of cash, but he kept losing alot too. I told him about micro trading while I was still learning my own system and approach. Bill I'm not ashamed to say came up with a hybrid of mine and his own, his new system he calls roulette. Roulette you may know is a highly disadvantageous game of chance, but in Bill's roulette the low float stock tricksters are the only disadvantaged. See Bill now goes and opens very low share orders in hundreds of these low float stocks. His orders have sell orders built in to sell if the stock goes up. Dozens of his orders stagnate doing not much of anything, but other dozens make 20% or 50% and even a few made more than 250% and a 1000%. His system preys on those that were like his former self.

There was a saying, there is no enemy worse to have than yourself. This saying is equally true with stock trading as in business where it is commonly taught in various forms. In stock trading many end up flocking, or grouping into certain niches. These niches help the less savvy learn and grow more proficient in an area of the market. Just as oil tycoons are experts in oil and tend to lose their rear ends in other fields, these traders get locked into a habit, a mold, a form that locks them down into predictable patterns. So who better could learn to profit off you, than you or someone else like you in the market?

Bill Bastour you're a hero in some fashion of mine now. He took my micro trading and made it better, and so can you. See even if your new, your inexperienced and a lightweight, trading will get easier with my simple micro trading approach. You'll learn a basic repeatable system to get started, practice it gaining ability and experience. While you do this you'll read and learn more skills in how others trade. At first you may or may not initiate these new ideas into your micro trading consciously, but you will do it. Some wont work well, some will. With each new experience, new and more capable ideas will be found out. Some of your incorporated ideas will prey on those that use the systems you learned about while still others will use the systems themselves to profit.

In this chapter lets now look at a basic starter you could learn to trade for quick profits in Bear and Bull markets. This system will always have a place in the market based on the history of the market so far. That history is old and has lasted through rise and fall of economies and nations, dying of technologies and birth of new ones that replaced them. This system could have been used before, during and after each World War, and all these little ones after. This system is so stable in its existence that it has weathered storms , crisis and assassinations of presidents.

The Panic Rebound-Play is what I will call it here. Now this wont work with falling rocks, or falling bricks, but works awesome with falling balls and even flipping cars...confused? Good.

Worse thing you could do is just rush out and try the *panic rebound play* before understanding it internally first. A rock falling will bounce, but it breaks when it does into pieces, same as companies falling from lots of different bad news sources or even a large dreadful news article. You *can* make money on these plays but lots and lots of market experience is needed. Now bricks falling don't bounce really, they crush and split, this is like companies going bankrupt or facing shut downs or sanctions, yes money *can be* made in these situations but that is for highly experienced traders and even then is the risk worth it when so many easier plays exist every day.

What a beginning micro trader is looking for is a good business that hit a speed bump to fast. This is like a company with strong growth but had a bad earnings report, or delay that wasn't anticipated. Some small thing that rocked the boat and got people shook to much for what the reality implied. So a few to many sold a little to fast and that took out those nasty *Stop-Loss* automatically traded orders. As those triggered maybe a few to many fell inline and the stock tanked, or entered what is called an oversold state. These happen pretty often due to stop loss orders and a little morning panic.

Company has opened same or higher for days or weeks, but earnings come out showing just a small tiny difference than anticipated, instead of a small sell off though the stock drops 15% in twenty minutes time. Yes this previous example happens, and happens a lot. This is actually a great example. Yet there is a bad example, one which to stay away from. A company has been steadily going up and begins to crash. No bad news. No reason. No if the drop happened at or shortly passed an easy number say like, 40.00 per share, or 12.50, or 10.25, that may be those nasty stop loss auto orders meant to keep you not only from losing to much but to take gains automatically if it reaches a certain point, see humans will use these types of numbers automatically, the whole dollar, the half dollar, quarter dollar are all mentally pleasing numbers, the only exception is the .99 and .89, both those can be seen as well due to familiarity of pricing. People go shopping and see those numbers a great deal at the end of the price so they may subconsciously choose such endings as well. So if this looks to have happened you can keep watching it but a play shouldn't be undertaken by a novice. The play that just starts tanking otherwise is probably a big Dump from a **Pump and Dump.** So stay back and move on to a more promising stock.

    Now the one we are looking for the drop is probably due to lazy traders who jumped onto the easy train bandwagon, bought stocks in companies that keep going up, but when they did they had ***bracket*** orders. This means the brokerage will sell it right off if drops again or has reached certain gain points, in this case. Now these types of multistage orders can and do have a place, and we both will be taking advantage of those who use it for wrong and right reasons. Don't kid yourself, trading is but one purpose, to take other peoples money while trying to keep others from taking yours. This makes it like any other trade or skill if you combined the euphoric high of a gambler into it.

Don't become that junky, looking for a fix. Keep it a job, keep it in proper perspective. By following these simple trading methods you can take money again and again, over and over again from the market. Investors are suckers for the most part. They just dump money into the market, anteing up, doubling down, tripling down. Many see their accounts grow huge over years of this, the compounding interest does do wonders.

Is it real though?

Some of these accounts so large they couldn't remove the funds(sell the stocks off) without causing tidal surges or even stock dumps from occurring, in turn dropping the paper gains as if they never existed. Paper gain suckers thrive in the investors world. Are you a paper gains junky or do you want real gains pulled out from other peoples accounts regularly?

So back to this awesome *panic rebound play*. Grabbing money from the market on rebounds will get easier and easier as the market prepares for huge retractions in the near future. The Big shots will be running like chickens with their heads cut off, they will try to become traders instead of investment strategists. All the while people like me, like you if you take the time to learn, will be shaving money off the market trade after trade as they cause swings to exaggerate. Try to look at the next two screenshots taken of the chart of a stock where this happened in a two day period.

Pictures have been reformatted for print, for full color please purchase the ebook edition.

As you can see in the first image….

Wait a second, I can almost hear that shouted and hate mailed my direction already. Many of you probably have no clue to what you just looked at. Don't worry I was in your shoes once before and I remember the struggle to get it, to understand charts and terms,etc. So instead of looking at those charts and talking about them, lets go into the next chapter and learn about charts.

3

In this chapter I am going to teach you how to read stock charts. I will be breaking down the key elements that you need to learn to successfully enter the world of trading. Now don't think you can skip this chapter. Reading a stock chart is more important than knowing how to fund your account to trade. Reading charts is so integral to a traders job that you cannot simply sign it off for later.

Johnny walks on over to the new car dealers office across town. He has dropped out of school having never learned to read well, and not being able to get away with bullying others to do his homework he felt it was time to just move on. Johnny is so excited though. Uncle Bubba, his mommas sisters husband, or possibly boyfriend, live in, has gotten him his first real job.

Now 6 months have gone by and Johnny saved his butt off because the sales agent said that even a new buyer can get approved for the Shelby Mustang if they saved that much and showed stable work history.

"Hey Danny, I brought the cash and pay slips". He looks around sees the same smiling faces all smiling at him. Such nice folks, he thinks, nothing like Bubba and Pops described.

"Come this way Johnny we got your car in back getting polished up, topped off with racing fuels, just kidding, just high octane fuel. Did you find a co-signer to help you out"?

"Danny you says I bring this much I wont need one those",Johnny says while waiving hundred dollar bills in a big fan that blocked out Johnny's whole face from view.

"Oh , with that much we can get you driving for sure", As Johnny's face was blocked from him so was his shrewd face blocked from Johnny's.

They walked to an office Johnny had never been in. "What's in this office", Johnny asks while wide eyed looking around at all the trophy's for top earner displayed around the room.

"Oh, this is my buddy Rod's office, he's the best as you can see from all the trophy's hes earned, he has been willing to take over and help you sign the paper work so you can get driving home instead of dreaming about it, you want the best helping you right"?

"Why of course the best has to be better then others at helping me to get driving faster, right?"

"They sure are! Hey Rod this is Johnny, you work your hardest and show him why your the best, ok!"

"Why thank you Danny. Hi! I'm Rod and I'll get you driving soon, Danny has told me all about the deal you guys cooked up and I am positive I can get you driving soon."

"Thanks Rod, Thanks Danny!" Johnny watches Danny walk out and turns back to Rod.

"Danny we got lots paperwork to go over, and I do apologize ahead of time but I will step out every now and then to take care of previous engagements, hope that wont bother you?"

"Oh no bother, Danny says your the best so your probably a busy guy huh!"

"Have you bought a car before Johnny, Danny has said its your first time ever?"

"Yes this is my first time, I mean, No I haven't bought a car before, I haven't ever owned one, borrowed Bubba's to get my license tested".

"Oh Bubba your boss helped you get your license tested did he, he must be a good boss."

"Oh yes sir, Bubba he helped me out a lot so far".

"Well you sit down right there Johnny and if you need anything don't worry I'll check in on you every now and then to make sure it is going ok. I have prepared all the paperwork, there is a great deal of it, due to your car choice, it is a fine choice a Shelby pick, your friends will be jealous."

"Oh they don't believe I'll get one, Tod's dad says I'm full of $#!t." Johnny looks at the stack, it has to be the largest stack of paperwork ever to be filled out. He remembers his teachers in high school collecting all the homework and that stack wasn't this large ever.

"Don't let the size of the stack fool you, it is easy to get through, everything is filled out where you check is *highlighted in pink and where you sign is highlighted in yellow, thumb print each page you sign with that ink pad so we can protect your identity, don't wont no druggies stealing it huh!"*

"They can do that Rod?"

"Sure can I seen it on that CSI T.V. show awhile back."

Wow Johnny thinks, he never thought that was real, just fictions. He looks ahead eyeing the paperwork and Rod as he exits the room. Rod had been wrong about the papers, the words he couldn't understand at all. Well he felt he understood sign here, and if you understand this check here and sign. Johnny glances up he's so sweaty and the room feels so stuffy. Only three pages through and so many to go, maybe he should just sign them he thinks, nah Pops says to read contracts is important. So back to trying his hand at reading.

"So hot!" Johnny couldn't help but say out loud, the room was definitively hot and stuffy. He is also so freaking thirsty, is there water. He looks around and sees none. *"Dam!"* He looks to the door, Rod is helping an old lady but he takes the time to send him a concerned look, standing up he comes walking back towards him.

"Johnny you ok, almost through reading your contracts and warranties?" Rod's smile is beaming and his eyes look so concerned Johnny thinks, this guy must be honest if he cares so much. *"I'm ok about done, do you think I can get a water when I am done it's gotten a little hot?"*

"Why sure Johnny of course I could do that for you,

I'll even get Judy looking into why the room warmed up ok!"

Johnny beams back that big ole smile Rod gives him, he just cannot help it, Rod is to nice a guy. *"Thanks Rod I appreciate your helping me so much!"*

Johnny watches him go and just starts flipping through checking and signing, oh man wait till his friends see his new ride, he pictures it with the top down, wind blowing through his hair, maybe even Maria his old crush would want him to give her a ride now, he grins thinking of the pun.

Finished finally Rod walks in with a water and another gentleman, who grabs up the monies and begins counting it all up. *"Johnny do you have full coverage insurance for the car?"* He asks Johnny while skimming through the paperwork.

"Uh I need that now? Bubba says you buy a car your allowed to go get it afterwards, Pops said it too even."

"Yes Johnny you can buy a car and go get it if you have insurance on another car, the insurance you already have will cover it in this state for up to 3 days to give you time to make the arrangements, do you have insurance on another car then?"

"Why no Rod, I told you its my first car why I have insurance on one if never had one before, does this mean I can't buy it?"

"Johnny, no way I will help you out, you already bought this car, everything is signed up and payment book

will be mailed, I'll let you come pick up the car next week after you brought in your proof of insurance."

"Next week, it's Tuesday Rod, next week thats a long time, I just bought it I wanna drive it bad."

"Calm down Johnny it's ok, your excited, it's just I have to release it because I am the sales agent that finalized this sale making me the responsible party and I have a wedding already planned to go attend, I took the time to help you, can you help me by waiting till I get back from Vegas?"

"Your going to Vegas for a wedding, whose, are they famous?"

"They are a little famous Johnny, my in-law is a former commercial model for the cable commercials not the radio obviously."

"Wow, well Rod I'm a little nervous, and stuff,but oh ok I'll be back Monday to get it then."

"Johnny Johnny I am sorry to do this but it needs to be Wednesday, but if that doesn't work we can rip this up, but the hit to your credit may make you not approved again for another 6 months, wouldn't want that to happen would we?

"SIX MONTHS, no SIR, I'll just come back Wednesday."

They shake hands and Johnny goes off to work the next day. He tries to keep it a secret but can't help telling everyone at one point or another throughout the day of his new car purchase.

"*So where is it?*" Some would ask, some asking while out right laughing. He would tell them he had to get insurance before he could go pick it up, he didn't say that he couldn't afford the policy quotes he was being offered for a shelby mustang. They all will see he thinks and tries seeing if Danny could find him insurance easier than he could, he did say he knew a great agent that got him a good rate.

So two days go by and the agent calls him up tells him a price for the car Danny sent the vin for, it was really low, wow not even a third what any others offered so he agreed to it and used his debit card to pay right there on the spot.

Wednesday

Johnny walks in and is ushered into Rod's office and asked to wait. He eventually shows a lady who comes in his insurance card and is handed more copies of the paperwork he signed previously and given the keys to his car.

"*We thought you would like it towed over so we had it arranged on the house because you've been such a good customer. Your car should be at your place now, so why are you still here!*"

"*I thought I would drive it home after I showed the insurance card!*"

"*Oh Sorry Danny left me with the impression you wanted to show it off as soon as possible. So thought I'd help you surprise them all. Hope I didn't cause any problems letting your friends and family see your car so* soon?"

"Well can I get going then I really want to get driving it?"

"Oh you get running home and if you need a mechanic remember we offer the best rates in town for cars purchased at this dealership."

"Mechanic, no way I wont beat my new car it will last a long long time."

Johnny races home and doesn't see any new Shelby, But the neighbors got one ugly Dodge parked outside. He goes in to call Danny and Rod because his cell went dead on the buss ride and walk home. His mother stops him and starts berating him.

"Are you stupid, are you so rich you can buy old towed in junkers now, what is wrong with you, what did you spend on that crap outside?"

"What are you talking about," He looks out the window and doesn't see his Shelby anywhere, "*I bought a Shelby Mustang, not some garbage mom.*"

"Shelby Mustang, I knew you couldn't read for $#!t, but didn't think you were completely stupid, you bought that junk Dodge Shelby turbo junker. It doesn't even have a motor. Your Pops called to see what it cost to get it going and its going cost more then thrice its worth you moron."

He doesn't hear anymore as he drifts outside, he kinda sways as he walks, maybe its because of the breeze, he walks around the rusty beat up dodge, Shelby it says and turbo, the rest of the badges had been broke off or fell off long before.

Thursday

Johnny finds out the hard truth, he owes a payment of 350$ a month on a broken down junk for the next 5 years and has lost his down payment of eight thousand dollars. All the lawyers said the same thing that he even bought insurance for that car make and model and vin, that he didn't complain about the car even it had been a week already since he bought it.

So what does that overripe long winded tale have to do with anything? Well short of it is, you'll be Johnny if you don't read charts, and other information correctly. Reading charts is a prerequisite to a trade, if you cannot read a chart, you cannot trade, only gamble. The chart isn't the only thing you need to read either on many plays that come your way. So many plays require reading SEC filings and other reports and news filings. Those may not be so important for this simple strategy I have included in this book, but charts and company news reports are.

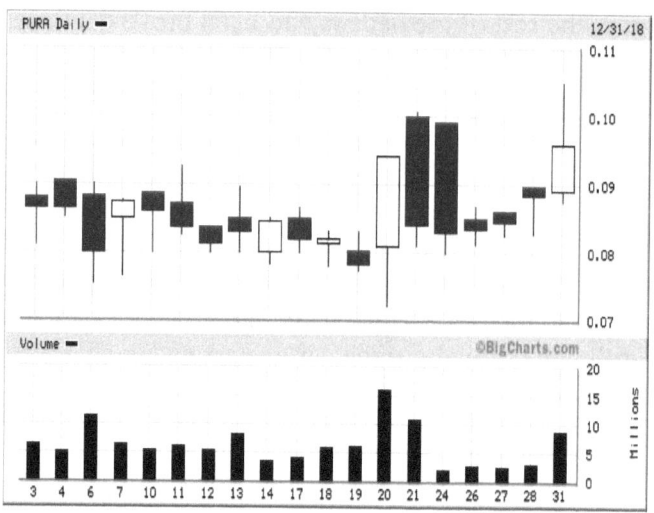

Pictures have been reformatted for print. For full color images please purchase the kindle ebook.

Notice in this last chart the upper left gives the ticker, and the chart timetable. PURA is the ticker, or what is used as a code to identify the company traded and the market it trades on. Daily is written next to it because the chart is a daily chart, it will show the high, the low, day open and day close price action.

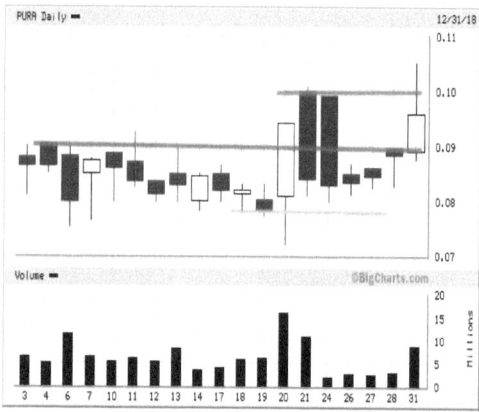

The Blue line represents earlier resistance levals. Notice the 2nd candlestick hit an invisible upper ceiling? Then It could not pass it for many days, but when it did it broke out and created a new resistance point. This new point is displayed in the color red. This breakout was a bad one though as you can see the old resistance did not make a new support point.

Notice the orange Line, this became the new support point, a point actually lower than before. Hint: Breakouts like this tend to be pumps or hype induced and will not last long, be weary.

The upper line is the RED line

The Middle Line is the BLUE line

The Lower Line is the Orange Line

Confused? Don't worry if you are, it is actually very simple. Each of those candles aligned in red and clear left to right represents a day of trading on this chart.

So from this chart the first high point would be the first resistance point. That resistance point just signifies a virtual wall that is pushing back on the stocks upper rising price capabilities.

Actually look back at that chart and see how it reached that high around .09 cents on the second day of trading listed, then each day after it struggled when it approached it?

That is it did till a volume surge took place. Oh I apologize, volume of trading is represented accordingly below each days trading.

Look at the 3rd day of trading shown, see the volume bar grow dramatically taller, black bar directly below? That is what kept the stock from plummeting. How do I know that just by the bar? I don't, I know it because of the candlestick and what it tells me to know. The candlestick shows massive sell-off happened that day to momentarily spike downward the price, see the wick far extend towards the bottom? The volume kept it from causing a big selloff. This was probably Pumped, or tipped by some one looking to profit. The tip or pump came and as the buyers came in they sold into them possibly with a market order. The volume also shows the hype was ongoing but a little cooled off over the next few days afterwards. So as the interest in the stock faded it eventually began to dump out the bottom. So 13 days in the boys got to pumping hard along with possibly a news piece, ok so I know that this was tipped and was with news during that period, seen both live with my two own eyes.

I'm using the chart to teach you to read them, don't judge me because its a Pump and Dump, I didn't pump it or alert it, plus eventually you will do what I did, and that's make money not off innocents being targeted, but by targeting the Pumpers in these schemes. But I am writing on Micro Trading not Pump and Dumper attacking so buy that book if I ever write it, that is if you like the idea of attacking scammers at the wallet and bank level.

So basically the resistance levels new and recent, are important to this simple strategy I am teaching you. Support levels are too, but these you should view going back 1 week, then again at 1mth, and 6mths, then 1 year. Looking at them singularly at each step going back gives a nice perspective of your risk levels.

So now you learned how to find support, and resistance levels, and what they mean. Now lets look at those candles again.

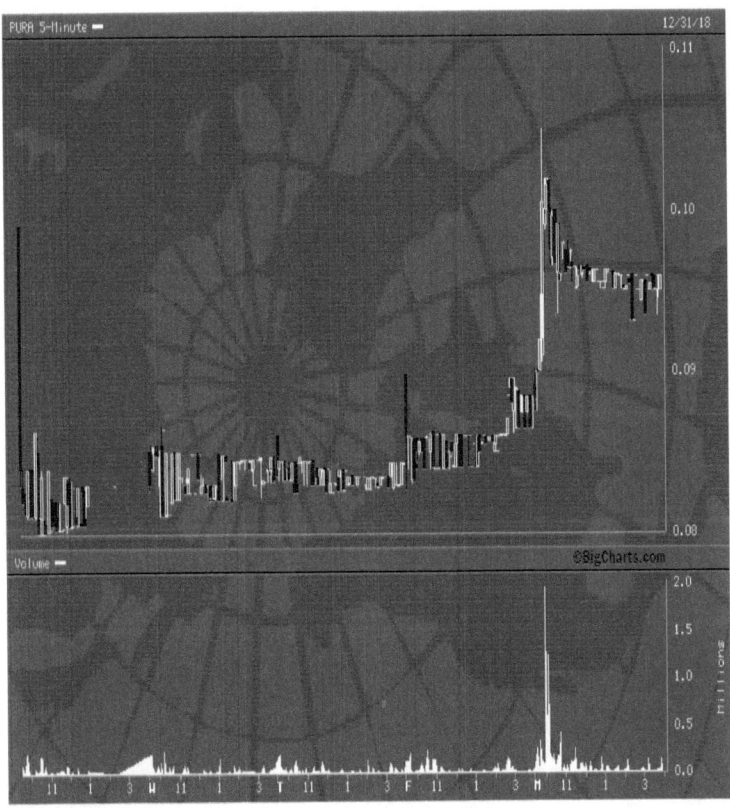

This all pictures were reformatted for print to keep costs down for the customers, but this picture actually shows how sometimes less is more. This picture actually becomes more easily readable at a glance under grayscaling.

Oh I am sorry that isn't the same style chart, or is it? This new chart uses a different background, yes, but is it different really?

Oh did you see it is a 5 minute chart, it does have a candle for every 5 minutes of trading instead of 1 for each days trading, wow that is tight in it's display too.

Can you still see the individual candles clearly? You should be able, but it takes effort to see them and decipher the information at the 5 minute level. This chart is good for a fast flow check of how the stock is flowing. You can very quickly see how it is moving and trending. But back to those candles.

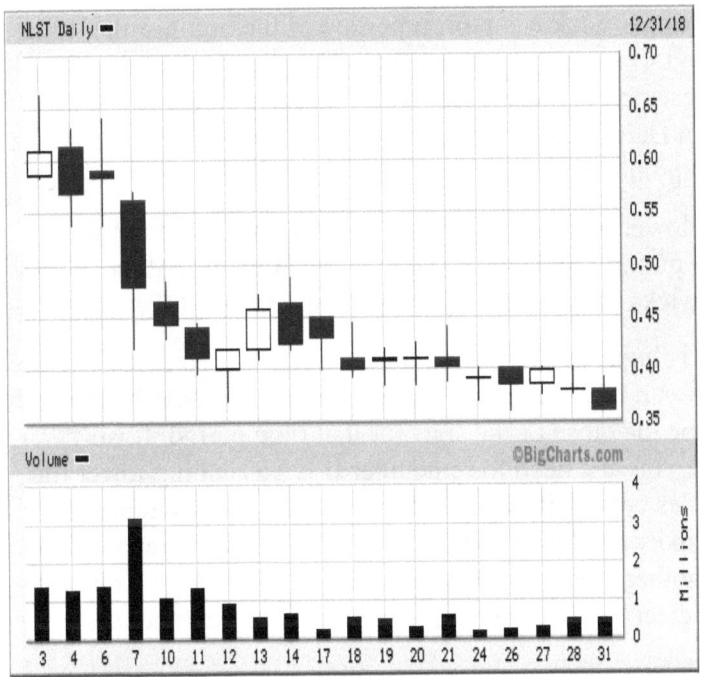

Do you see the candle body shape? And do you see the upper and lower wick?

The upper wick is a representation of the high for that time period. If a 5 minute chart, then that wick at the top represented highest price during that 5 minutes of trading. If it is a Daily representation then that upper wick is the daily high point of trading.

The lower wick shows the lowest price it traded for at that time period represented. So low and High of that day is in the wicks low and high points. Pretty easy right?

Top is high, lower is low, not too complicated is it? But, the body can be a bit more confusing, see the candle body upper can be the close or the start for that time period. It isn't hard, you just need to remember if it was ending lower the candles color will represent that it fell during that period, and likewise that if it ended higher it would be represented in another color. Or, if you looked at that 5 minute chart it was clear candle and color candle as representations.

So always check which color candle represents open low close high, and open high close low. Once you have the different candles figured out then it is very easy. Even the figuring out is pretty easy to figure out, but still important nonetheless.

So if price is trending up the lower body represents the open of that time period. Likewise the top of the candle body would thereby indicate the close for that time representation.

On the other hand if that candle represents trending downward, or falling prices during that time period. Then the Lower body of the candle would represent the close, and the upper the opening.

Quick exercise, just to make sure you got it, look at the next chart and mark each candle as up, or down depending on whether it displays a candle that's showing rising price action or lowering of price action.

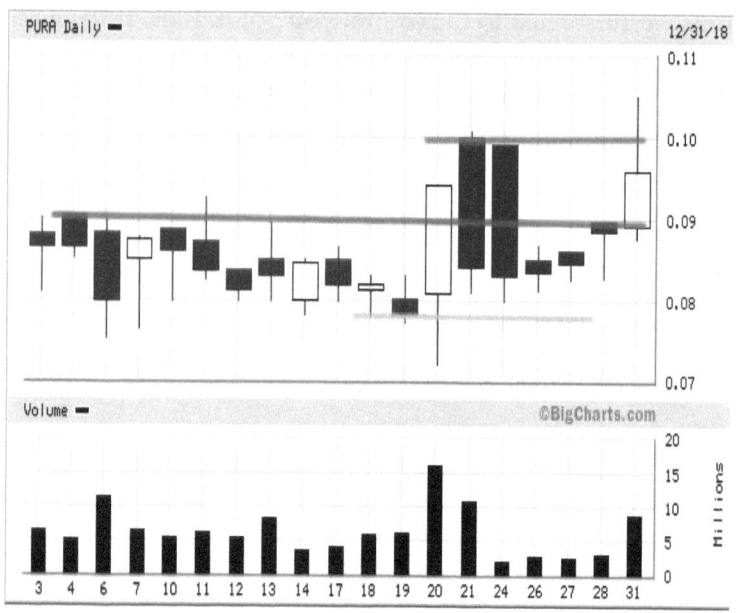

Red Candles represent ?

Clear represent?

Look closely do the red days trend positive overall and the clear negative? That is the fastest wat to check which is which.

In this case red is positive days, and clear is negative days.

Solid candles were RED

Hollow candles were Clear

Upper line was RED

Middle line was Blue

Lower line was Orange*

So did you pick red as up and clear as down? I hope so the answer was pretty available to you in the picture. If not, please reread and try again but on earlier charts. Maybe watch a Youtube video on it or better yet take my Udemy course on Microtrading. This book coupled with the course is far better than either of them apart. Video really helps teach on subjects like this better than simple pictures ever could. But, books are fabulous learning mediums in there own right, and have the ability to be easily reread and gone back to when needed. Be confident that this book will teach you what is necessary to Microtrade effectively when taken seriously.

So at this point you can read a basic candlestick chart. If you want to read other charts I could recommend an upcoming book I am publishing called "Stock", that book will be more comprehensive like a Bible on the subject. For the beginner though this Microtrading is enough to get you trading in the green regularly if used intelligently. Mind you common sense does play a role, if the markets are crashing on Tuesday and you think rebounds are going to work against a tidal wave Tsunami sell off, well you need a mental health check.

The overall markets, and World and in some cases local news plays a role sometimes small, sometimes large, in the world of stocks. During these Big events or Direct affecting events where it isn't clear how it could affect the stocks involved, Don't play around, just don't trade till it becomes clear. Now if your confident and have experience you can then think about playing the riskier times and the riskier moves. Right now, your goal is to learn, first on the easy, then move up expanding your horizon with the growth of your trading accounts profits. To often traders new to the field want to be fully experienced speculating geniuses at every kind of market, and in every style of trade. Don't think this way. Take trading like motor vehicle skills. You first learned to crawl, then walk, then run and skip, even jumping at the same time. Eventually you got a trike, or big wheel, then a bicycle with training wheels. Trading is the same, just as with little aptitude you could successfully travel about, you ***can start trading profitably*** if you stick to the simpler methods. Master them till your proficiency is well established. Then learn another method or two, mastering it before moving on. Doing this it isn't unreasonable that you could keep up a pace of learning that in 5 years you can do 5-15 types of trades in half of the major market conditions, and make many many dollars in profits. That would be the day your equivalent to a bicycle rider with no training wheels.

Common sense is a valuable asset. If you don't have it, this may not be for you. Yet it still might, many successful traders suck at common sense but are crazy masters in Stock trading so in the end you have to make your decisions, and those will be your own. I wont be responsible of your choices, just like you wont be of mine.

Now you may be asking, where did I get these charts. That's easy, the internet, and mainly I get charts off of Bigcharts. They have many features and abilities with drawing you up an accurate chart fast and free. Another place for Charts is at Chartmill. They have charts with a screener/scanner.

Now that gets me to the next big tool for your arsenal. See how are you to find trades, these stocks in play don't usually call you up and say hey buddy buy my shares long and you'll gain big on your bottom line this week. So how do you find them? You find them the way most traders do! You need to use scanners to find the ones that are fitting into your criteria. Now if you could search for all aspects of a great potential trade setting up, then execute on them instantly-automatically in a micro portion of milliseconds, well you would be a Hedge fund manager making billions off that, but you can't, probably can't. So you need to find the potentials before they trigger the last prerequisite, and be ready to trade them if they do hit the final requirements. So scanners should become your best friends. Why, because they will bring you the stocks in play in time for you to catch them and trade them.

4

Stock Screeners/Scanners are the scouts. In the military during a war the big shots send out scouts to gather intel so they can make decisions effectively and reliably. In trading it is a war, a war to get other peoples money in your account, and not yours into their accounts.

These scanning tools help you screen out the fluff, weeds, silt, whatever you want to identify it as, garbage, from the valuable potential gems, diamonds, and gold, the possible winner plays. These tools will only show what you ask them to show though. So understanding them for this type of trade is going to be a priority of yours if you expect to acquire stocks in play before the plays are over.

When a stock has already played out, that's it. Getting in then is just a mistake, a mistake commonly called FOMO, or the fear of missing out. This one bad mistake has caused traders to literally kill themselves. Suicide because they traded fearing they would miss an opportunity and traded a play already over, or never going to play out to begin with. Losing life savings, their homes cars etc, after entering trades as a gambler, not a trader.

Speculation is not gambling, it is math, and experience combined to create opportunity to profit. Human nature is predictable, and highly so. This leads to historical repetitions that can be acted upon when the cycle of the action is coming back around.

If the stock market reacts to an announcement of war the same way every time it is announced, that doesn't mean it always will. But, it does mean that the odds are stacked highly that it will. If oversold stock, stock not just oversold, but sold to much to fast reacts historically time and time again the same way, well that means you have a potential opportunity. Knowing this common reaction, you can look for the action and when it happens use that knowledge of what will most likely occur to profit.

If a president keeps saying that they will deregulate and increase energy production, and you know they have been acting out their other rants pretty well. Then you need to profit off that, you'll know fuels will drop at retail in the future. You could then sell at those higher prices currently and cover at the lower prices of the future.

Now those are fictional examples and in no way a trading advise. Nothing in this book is a particular trade advise, they when given are only examples for reference. Lawyers…ugh…

Back to the scanners. Scanners can be used in more ways than could be written in even a single encyclopedia set. So obviously I would not landslide you with all the ways you wont even need in the beginning. I will teach you what you need to know now and probably a lot extra due to my ADHD nature.

Scanners are the tool you need to develop a watchlist. This watchlist helps you to tackle stocks at the right timing. So think of a watchlist like a menu at a restaurant. The menu tells you what is available for consumption, the watchlist tells you what is priming for being a stock in play. Watchlists come in two basic varieties for us concerning your beginners level. General watchlist and a active watchlist. The general watchlist is stocks you've traded, and are active priming for a future possible play. This general list keeps them in the radar for when they become active. The Active list is that days, or weeks active stocks in play.

See stocks go active and in many cases offer more than one opportunity to profit, missing the first, don't worry. No need to FOMO, just watch it for the next play that comes. It may not, but you'll know that when volume fades or no real action keeps up. In the beginning do not put more then a single handful of stocks on your active list and I think no more than twenty to fifty on your general list.

At first if your new you'll be slower and need more time to notice the movement that your waiting for. Having few means less plays coming your way, but also means more attention to catch any one that does. In the beginning you'll probably catch your play from stocks not even on your lists, but still make them. Making them is like doing Kata's in martial arts, it prepares you for when you need to use those moves in a real fight.

Some tips are to look for increased volume, an example would be one and a half times more volume, and price drop or gain over 5%.

Price action approaching 26 or 52 week lows, or the highs respectively. The higher number of stocks being scanned the slower the results will be. Have you ever scanned your whole PC for viruses? Have you scanned a downloaded file or just a few folders on your PC? These experiences should help you comprehend what I mean by speed differences. If your scanning the whole market scan just for two or three points. Nearing 52 week highs, higher volume than normal, that be a good scan for general market. But putting 29 points in a scan and scanning the whole market would be slow for most peoples systems and net ability, if done on all the market or a large section of it. So for finer scans of more detail, do it on your watchlists.

Now I know I didn't go into lots of details but you really don't need to be overwhelmed right now. Success will come from being an expert in simplicity and accuracy. So remember where we got cut off a while back on how to trade a simple rebound play? Yes, the one where you needed to read the charts.

Don't remember then go back and read on that one more time, you'll be surprised at how much more you get out of it. So for this play you will just need to look for big droppers after a recent spike or long good price increase of many days.

Running the scanner you'll find many but you'll want only the ones very recent in dropping, and check the News on them. Most Broker accounts give you news access for the stock your viewing, look at it fast. No major news caused the drop? Good now check for it to hit lower support.

Is it rebounding off the support? Well to check that it is you'll need to check Level2 fast. After Level2 confirms buyers are beginning to outweigh sellers, you'll know. Oh, did I do it again? I am most assuredly not sorry. See some of you know Level2 and will already now be looking for these plays, not recommended, but some of you will have no clue as to what I am saying. For the clueless I will teach you Level2 reading in the next chapter. Well I will teach you what to look for for this play in the next chapter.

So those who know, well you see the bounce starting, buy, that simple.

But, don't buy to much, this is microtrading after all. The benefits of microtrading is it is easier to profit in many ways. One such way is that very small orders get executed fast, if done right.

The other reason is your not needing to overcome trading commissions/fees. So say a stock drops 23% and begins to bounce/correct itself. Stock may not even reach back to within 15% of its former glory on the rebound, may take a week or day, even a year to get back completely.

So if that stock was 10$ a share it is at around, mental clicks and humming, $7.70 a share.

The bounce might only hit 8.50 the first day and only 8.10 or 8.20 on the direct rebounding.

If your broker was standard Like Etrade or TdAmeritrade you would pay out more then 6$ to buy shares, and more then 6$ to sell them again.

That's over 12$, not to mention if you had three buy orders done to fill and 2 to sell it could add up fast. At the single in and out you would need near a thousand shares and near perfect take on the trade to just cover the fees. Since to cover the fees is so bad to make the risk vs reward worth it you would need over 5k shares in this trade to even seem worth it. Less would be to risky and you would find yourself losing money like many traders more often than not.

But!

No fee trading on micro level with say you have 50$ grand total in your account, you would buy 1 share at a limit order. Realistically limit .10 above the market and buy 1 share. So you get in at say 7.90$ a share at one share. You put your single share back up for sale instantly for 8.05 or 8.10.

Now if it spikes even momentarily then drops you will most likely have it sold anyway since its just one share.

Congratulations fictional microtrader you just made .15 cents. Not much, I know, but your goal is at first to gain experience buying and selling profitably. Not a goal to become overnight millionaires.

By doing the quick profit at first you'll lock in more pluses faster on these volatile stocks. In two weeks you could easily have your account of 50$ at a good healthy Charles Schwab jealous making 55-60$, or 10% or more in gains. Once you have 5$ or more up you can risk that 5$ on trying to make a bigger jump, say .25-.50 cents on a 5 dollar to 10 dollar stock.

Oh that is not all. Once you hit double and have 50$ to ride on in cushion, you could play aggressive if you desired and go for the bigger stocks that have a single simple bad news like slightly less earnings or just fell 20% or more. So now you have say a 20$ stock that fell 20% and is rebounding. You bought 2 shares, at 33$ catching it just above bottom on the rising side.

You hold placing a more aggressive sell order in just for a possible spike home-run catch of say 18.50 a share.

You watch the ticker, price up up, down, down, up,up,up,dn,up it goes. Level2 starts show possible wall at 18.40 develop so you change your order and sell on limit at 18.35 your two shares. The executions fast but you see a wave of buyers and stock rips back up to 19.22 before stalling.

Forget about it!

You made your gains real the moment you took them when it looked possible to reverse again.

Be proud not discouraged. You just made money. You made 3.70$ no fees to share. You also made more than 10% on that single trade. Yes its a few dollars, a Starbucks coffee, a cheap Mcdonalds sandwich and coffee but you made it. To some of you that few dollars could make a world of difference too. In a country like the Philippines that is more than many make in a whole day working.

Don't get discouraged of the small amount to those that don't need to start small. You people would love to jump in with 10k or 5k or even 100k and probably lose most if not all of it very quickly in the stock market. No, then learn this method first. Build your trading experience with perfect trades, learning from *SMALL losses* instead of hundreds or thousands in losses you might lose ,20 cents, or even a dollar if you two left thumbs an order and it goes market instead of limit, Robinhood will screw you every time on those.

What is your ultimate goal? If it is to be successful then here you go, the dollar will turn to five, then ten,, then fifty, then eventually thousands. I know real life examples of this, and have proven my own system with myself and complete stock noobs.

Sally(what I will call her here)took 10 minutes and me trading twice like this till she took over found Chico's dropping and made 18% on a 3 stock buy and sell. Her first trade. She even could answer what she expected it to do and where she would try to sell.

Will you necessarily gain your first trades? No, but you will learn faster if you really read this book and take these simple methods to heart mind and body. This is the easiest type of trading you can do from all the types I have tried I can really say that. I shoot a hundred percent on the rapid fire approach putting in my sell as soon my buy is executed. I shoot over 98% on the holding for a little more approach. That is awesome, my biggest loss was .70 cents on a two thumb mistake, where I hit the order type to change back to market as I put to buy. It was a mistaken trade, I wasn't meant to be in like that so I sold immediately and took the loss, if I had held I would been up. But That would been gambling. That was my only loss in Microtrading.

Your almost ready to get out there, lets learn those level2's.

5

Did some of you already try trading with your Robinhood accounts yet? Well if you messed up jumping in a little to soon don't worry we are going to learn some more important stuff to make it easier. Under my first outline I had planned to make the "Stocks in Play" my next focus for a chapter, but as many people who write have found, things pop up. So for now we will go briefly into how to read the Level2 in regards to this simple strategy.

Level2 is in simple terms a chart that shows the purchase orders and sell orders that are going on. Now that is an over simplistic explanation but it is easily understood and all that really matters at this moment. What you need more importantly to understand is how to read it when attempting a rebound play.

So first I will give some advice, find some plays before trading them. Just mentally trade them and watch these level2's and try to predict the shift from sell off to buy up or vice versa. Getting reasonably well at seeing the shift before trading will increase your effectiveness.

TLRY

| ews | Ratings | **Level II** | Options | Soc |

Tilray, Inc. - Class 2 Common Stock NASDAQ
$84.80 **-0.81** (0.95%) B **84.80** A **84.98** Vol **4,128**
01/17/2019 08:22:58 ET

MPID	Shares	Bid	Ask	Shares	MPID
NSDQ	38	84.81	84.98	100	ARCX
EDGX	300	84.80	84.98	29	NSDQ
ARCX	100	84.50	85.20	100	EDGX
BATX	200	82.98	108.03	100	TRLN
TRLN	100	60.72	199,999.99	100	MZHO
MZHO	100	0.01			

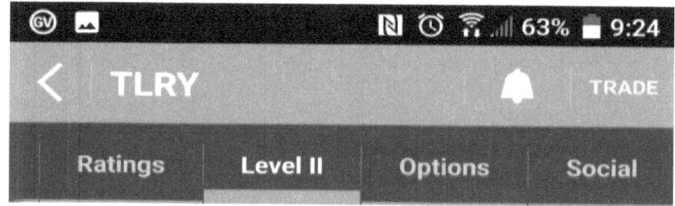

The previous two images are off screenshots of me checking level2 premarket, yes time shows 9:24 but that is P.M and in the Philippines not the US of A.

This Ticker can be troublesome, acts like a pennystock pumper half the time. Still with experience and this Microtrading it becomes fairly easy to make large gains repeatably.

Next we will start breaking down the level2 chart.

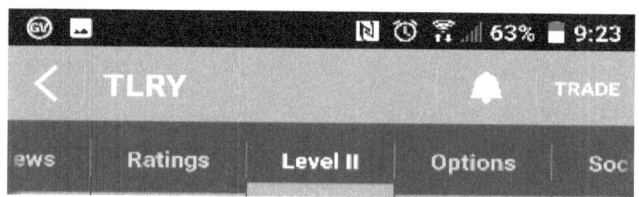

MPID	Shares	Bid	Ask	Shares	MPID
NSDQ	38	84.81	84.98	100	ARCX
EDGX	300	84.80	84.98	29	NSDQ
ARCX	100	84.50	85.20	100	EDGX
BATX	200	82.98	108.03	100	TRLN
TRLN	100	60.72	199,999.99	100	MZHO
MZHO	100	0.01			

Highlighted in Yellow is the Bidders, or the ones with purchase orders outstanding. NSDQ 38, **EDGX 300**, ARCX 100. See those representations are the who and the amount of volume wanted. 84.81, 84.80, 84.50 is the dollar amount per share offered.

As You can see here I'm showing the buyers side.

The Circled was the Yellow*

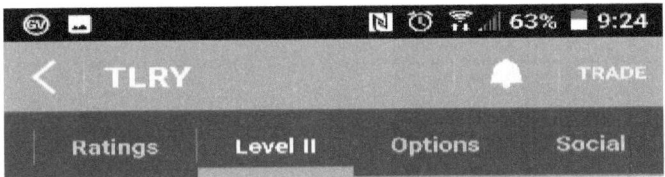

MPID	Shares	Bid	Ask	Shares	MPID
EDGX	100	84.90	84.98	100	ARCX
NSDQ	38	84.81	84.98	29	NSDQ
ARCX	100	84.50	85.20	100	EDGX
BATX	200	82.98	108.03	100	TRLN
TRLN	100	60.72	199,999.99	100	MZHO
MZHO	100	0.01			

Here in Blue is the seller que. It's displayed mirrored on this chart style but not always. Same General info except reversed. Now the volume and price is for sell offers in que. If you noticed this level2 chart is moments after the other one was taken, see the differences?

As You can see here I'm showing the seller side.

Circled was the Blue*

If you looked above the highlighted info and noticed the small volume of 4,128, that is indeed low and would make it not something I would be interested in during Market hours, but these were taken before market open and lower volume is standard. I'll post 2 charts on the past trading, take a look.

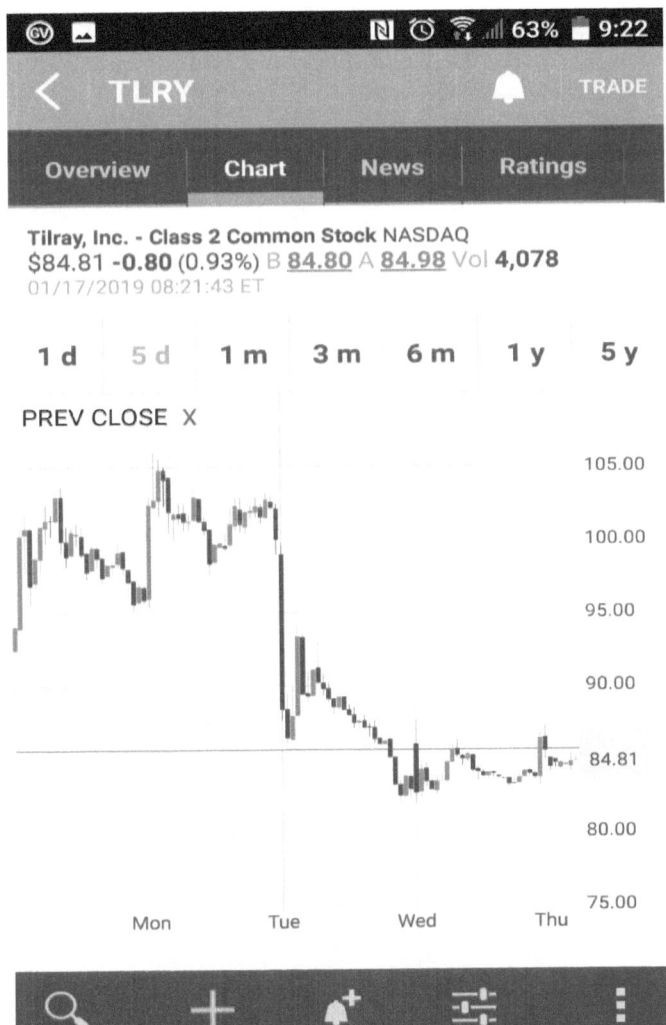

5 day chart.

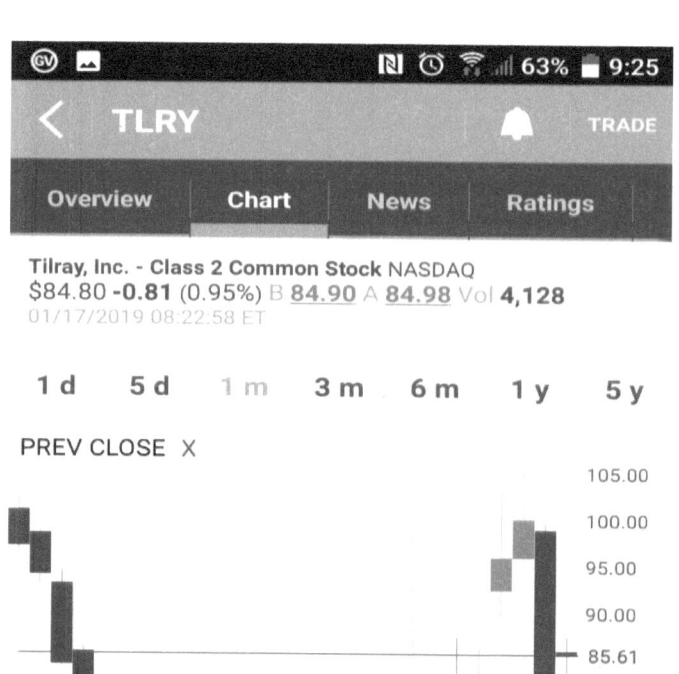

1 month chart.

Notice in the 5 day the stock had been hit hard, but looking at the month chart it looks more like a failed breakout or consolidation occurring. On the 1 month chart take a look, the price action premarket is just above established support levels. Without good news or some Hype I think this stock will stray down if it doesn't rally at today's market open. I am not always right, this is just a speculative view based on experiences built on watching the market. Also if you look into the News you would see what looks like favorable news at first, but then closer reading shows what looks like a backroom deal in hiding. 350million, 100million of which paid now or soon to another business to work together. Yet *up to a minimum of 10million paid each year for 10 years. Basically meaning they may get a minimum of a 100 million over that period of time, but not necessarily. That means a potential substantial net loss on the deal. Mind you the payouts not only not covering the deal money put up but TLRY will also be incurring costs the whole time supplying the product for this other business. Looks almost like a real backroom deal insurance policy in case the Markets don't work out favorably long-term. What better way for insiders to make sure they make bank long term no matter the circumstance. Ok, Ok, so I lean towards paranoia, but you would too if you sat with men and woman who run these big companies like I have. Cutthroats all of them. Enron wasn't alone, The big banks in the Real estate collapse were not alone, this is common. Disclosure though is that TLRY and Authentic could and probably are ok so don't just run around scared selling off, why, because I am not shorted on it yet. Just Kidding!

I wont edit the previous statement, so we both will see how it works out, either way it isn't a favorable position for me in microtrading or in my day/swing trading accounts.

Ok so trading opened and I took screenshots for you here is a bunch.

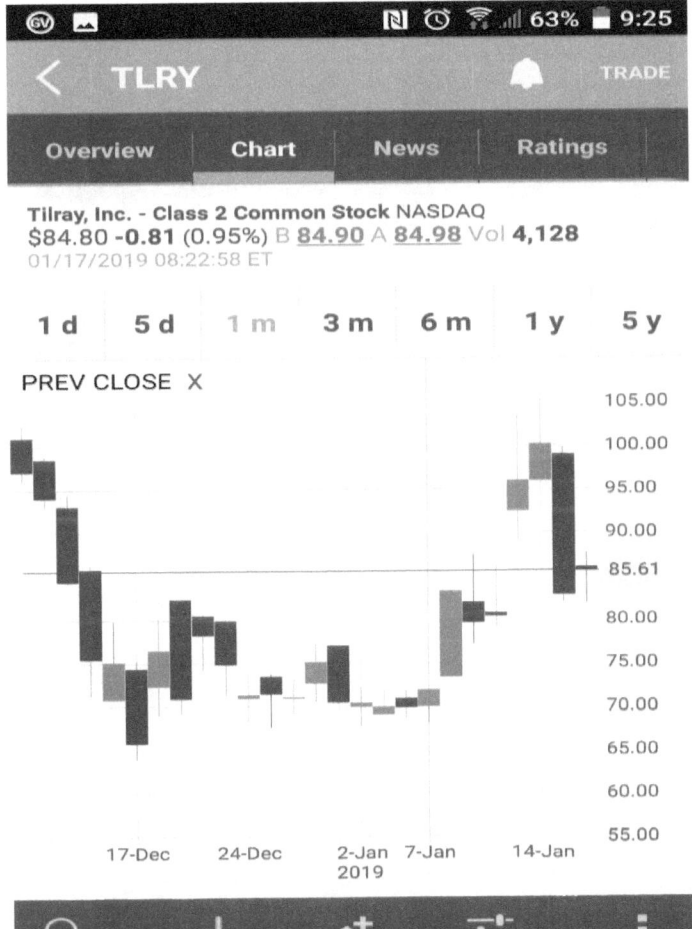

Right before open….hmmm

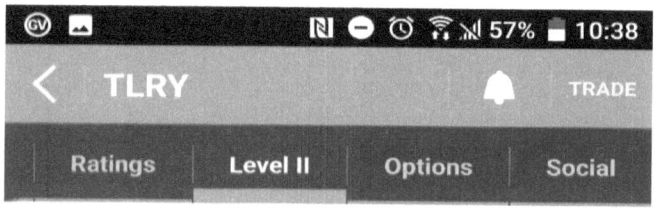

MPID	Shares	Bid	Ask	Shares	MPID
NSDQ	150	82.90	82.99	200	EDGX
EDGX	100	82.76	82.99	200	NSDQ
ARCX	100	82.71	82.99	100	CINN
BATX	100	82.57	83.32	100	BATX
EDGA	100	82.47	83.59	100	ARCX
BATY	100	82.46	83.67	100	NYSE
NYSE	100	82.05	85.27	200	BOSX
AMEX	100	82.04	85.29	100	BATY
PHLX	300	81.82	85.31	100	EDGA
GSCO	1,000	81.70	85.39	100	AMEX
BOSX	100	81.53	85.44	1,700	PHLX

Dammm She's tanking so far, so I Checked for any good news releases, nothing good.

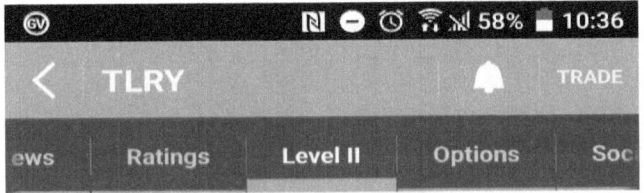

Tilray, Inc. - Class 2 Common Stock NASDAQ
$82.76 **-2.85** (3.33%) B 82.60 A 82.99 Vol **180.3K**
01/17/2019 09:36:23 ET

MPID	Shares	Bid	Ask	Shares	MPID
NSDQ	445	82.60	82.90	1	NSDQ
EDGX	200	82.51	82.98	200	PHLX
ARCX	1,200	82.50	82.99	100	MWSE
BATX	100	82.31	83.00	100	BATX
BATY	100	82.30	83.43	100	CINN
CINN	100	82.30	83.43	100	IEXG
EDGA	100	82.14	83.50	1,500	ARCX
AMEX	100	82.04	83.69	100	NYSE
NYSE	100	82.04	85.00	300	EDGX
IEXG	100	82.00	85.23	100	EDGA
PHLX	300	81.82	85.27	200	BOSX

Might look for a bounce if it continues anymore.

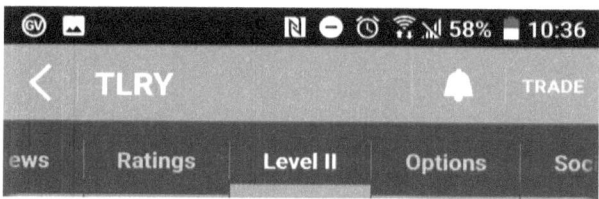

MPID	Shares	Bid	Ask	Shares	MPID
NSDQ	1	82.75	82.90	1	NSDQ
CINN	100	82.62	82.99	100	EDGX
MWSE	100	82.62	82.99	100	MWSE
EDGX	200	82.51	83.00	100	BATX
ARCX	1,200	82.50	83.43	100	CINN
BATY	100	82.30	83.43	100	IEXG
BATX	100	82.29	83.50	1,500	ARCX
EDGA	100	82.29	83.69	100	NYSE
AMEX	100	82.04	85.23	100	EDGA
PHLX	300	81.82	85.27	200	BOSX
GSCO	1,000	81.70	85.29	100	BATY

Microtrading on this, might not pull much but with the hectic bounces instantly I don't mind scalping a quick profit.

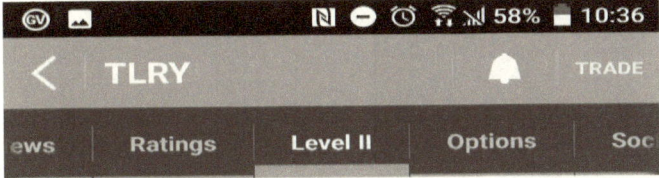

Tilray, Inc. - Class 2 Common Stock NASDAQ
$82.69 **-2.92 (3.41%)** B 82.60 A 82.99 Vol **181.1K**
01/17/2019 09:36:30 ET

MPID	Shares	Bid	Ask	Shares	MPID
NSDQ	495	82.60	82.90	1	NSDQ
ARCX	100	82.60	82.98	200	PHLX
EDGX	200	82.51	82.99	100	MWSE
BATX	100	82.32	83.00	100	BATX
BATY	100	82.30	83.43	100	CINN
CINN	100	82.30	83.43	100	IEXG
EDGA	100	82.14	83.50	1,500	ARCX
AMEX	100	82.04	83.69	100	NYSE
NYSE	100	82.04	85.00	300	EDGX
IEXG	100	82.00	85.23	100	EDGA
PHLX	300	81.82	85.27	200	BOSX

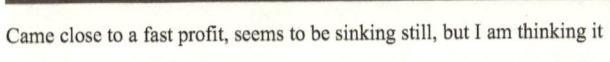

Came close to a fast profit, seems to be sinking still, but I am thinking it will rebound soon into the 83's.

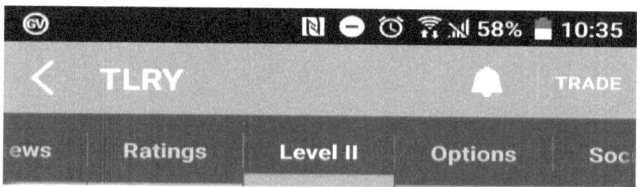

It's happening, right there folks that is not a play for noobies, but get some experience and you'll see it happening based on historical and math speculation. Syke thats a little older pic...wait for the real deal it will happen, time for more screenshots, be right back.

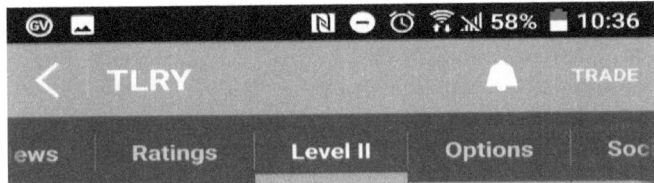

Buys are starting to bounce see the volume surging on buy side? Possibly some shorts covering or the new low just looks too good to some watching like me.

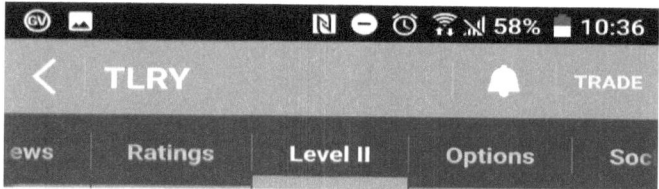

Wait for it, I see it coming, see the buy volume starting to out weigh the sell line by line? Modern Trading almost reminds a person of the bucket shop trading of old. For those that do not know the reference, you will learn about it.

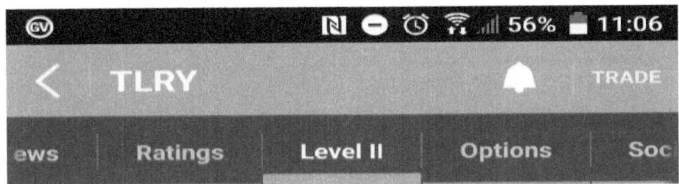

Better than I had thought...dam good job, glad I didn't sell on .15 cents fast profit, the little extra tanking gave me time to make my plan and go for dollars.

Low stress trading and easy profits. This is sniper style trading, aiming small but getting way more accuracy. Making 2$ with an account at 100$ doesn't sound like much but that happened over a half hour time frame roughly. Also doing these trades like this, learning with small accounts got me learning faster and more profitably than learning with a traditional account the average Joe or Jane would have opened.

Now folks, don't you want to learn smarter, faster, and more profitably? Don't you wanna claim membership in the 5% profitable traders club? If the other ways worked for the average Joe or Jane more people would have found success. They haven't found it though and thank God they haven't, because now we can learn how to strategically cash in off of them, day after day. Immoral? No Way! All of life is about profiting off someone else, whether it be profiting off the people who made your tv by watching televisions shows on it, or profiting off the restaurants workers, or profiting off of your own workers at your own business. Learning to profit off folks trading in the market is Darwin's on philosophy, survival of the fittest.

Are you ready to get going? Then don't forget the next short chapter before you do.

Then stop listening to these Gurus, and tipsters, and pumpers, they want to hook you in and eventually take your money. Learn to trade on your own terms, with less risk, and more rewards to be had. If this book left you with questions feel free to look me up on Udemy and get my course on Microtrading, it should be up relatively at the same general time as the book, within a week I am hoping and planning for within a few days.

6

    Finally back on track, Stocks in Play it is. You may have heard me use this term. May have read it or seen it or heard it other places to. It is an important term and doesn't have much behind it as far as details to what it is. Stocks in Play is exactly that, the stocks that are in play. These stocks are more active and more set up, ready to be picked through for your moves. Earlier we saw some ways to pick out a stock that is in play. Now we wont go back much into how to pick out or find these Stocks that are in play. More at this point would only be confusing.

    Last chapter while writing and just checking the market for a good level2 chart I found a play and profited live while writing. Wasn't as nice as seeing a video of me trading it but it is the same in the end, you saw as you read this the real time play by play action, except here I snuck an old picture as a joke in the middle. Still laughing but got to, this been way to serious last few months planning and plotting and writing this book up. Lot of work, it may be small but it is direct without all that extreme excess fluff many books and courses have. I also wanted something small enough that it worked like a handbook in the beginning. I have kept that goal of teaching what needs to be known to make simple repeatable profitable trades. Now it is up to you. So for the Stocks in Play, Robinhood on the desktop/amazon fire site you will see a short list of big movers updated almost like real time. Well mine is set up that way right from the get go so yours should be too. If it is that is really all you need to find stocks in play at the beginning. So along with Stocks in Play I will teach you few extra tips before I say good bye and thank you for taking the time to learn with me, hope to see you in my course, those who sign up the first 30 days the course is up and send me a message with them holding up my book will get a surprise freebie. It might be up to an hour of live via chat or voip etc, depends on my location and yours and ability of access at the time, coaching. Getting to trade with me will definitely speed up the curve if you're a little slower than average.

1st tip is to be prepared, be up a minimum 1 hour before the market opens, be reading and looking through news releases and general market talk before it opens by a minimum of half an hour. If you want to find the easiest targets.

2nd Run your scanners as soon as you wake up, yes even before your morning tinkle if your only waking up an hour before open you will want to have this going as soon as possible.

3rd Don't feel rushed to trade, get to where you don't feel a need to trade, just look and react if a REAL PLAY appears before you. Remember FOMO or as explained earlier the fear of missing out will break you, you don't want that. So just trade the REAL plays, not just anything and pretend it is a play-that would just be gambling.

4th you see the big drop of a play, check your charts going back as taught in this book earlier, then check level2, wait for the rebound points and watch for them, do not trade till they show rebounding occurring at those points or above them, if below, skip that trade being wrong on where the rebound is means the trade is not speculation anymore but out right dice throwing. Yet It rebounds the way you forecasted, hit buy on your already typed up order, then instantly put order for a reasonable amount more on limit and send it off. Better to take an instant profit while still learning than possibly miss it and not get out before a false rebound collapses.

5th Take my course on this topic and learn more with videos and lectures. Much more to learn and definitely more plays to be played. While Udemy is a lifetime access capable too so like this book you can go back and learn more and more as you grow more and more capable, because of that I will be teaching way more on that platform than on here.

6th Don't try learning lots of other methods right away. Yes learning is good but drowning in info isn't. Learn something truly before moving on. A simple tip, learn one play till you double your account, then more to the next one, learn it till you double your account again. As you progress doubling becomes more and more harder in terms of the amount to be doubled, but, you will also have more and more wisdom and experience so it should stay only slightly off flatline in terms of time it takes to double each time.

7th review this book full stars, don't be stingy. I will probably make less than minimum wage on this project, that is if you the one I am teaching a valuable tool, doesn't do your part. As an ebook author I depend on your positive reviews and online recommendations to places like book groups on Facebook or Stock chat groups you've joined. My first book I didn't put as much into it as I wanted, but I still put nearly 10k in minimum wage labor, since I knew the odds were it wouldn't sell a hundred copies I didn't edit it and love on it the way I really wanted. Just wasn't feasible. But that book made a steady sales rate. Just averages around 30$ in profit a month, but because I keep my word , and because I said I would do better if it actually sold over a hundred copies on the next books and would also rework that older one and offer it again with richer content. Yet that also depends on you, I need good reviews they take but a moment. If I get them and if the books take off the prices will also drop. I am not writing to get rich, I already am getting rich trading day by day. I am writing this to teach others and also pass forward the love through charity. So here is a tip, want real content and authors to work harder for you? Give them good reviews, and feedback.

Email me @ tordynamics@gmail.com if you want, I will try to make time to help you out, thanks, and Good day!

Sean Michael G.

Will the adventure continue . . .

Follow the adventures of My family and I as we travel the world making money out of thin air, yes out of thin air. Oh alright so not out of thin air…..but it feels that way.

Hope you gave positive reviews, and recommendations to others.

If you have any ideas on how to make my work better, please send me constructive criticism. Can be anything from layout to grammar, but be easy with grammar it is my nemesis. I have taken a half dozen of college writing classes just to improve to this point, and this isn't that good. I still struggle. Don't ask me why it is so hard for me to get it, maybe I was meant to be Japanese or German lol. Yet I know many more fans will help me to grow especially as I teach them valuable skills to improve their lives at the daily level. Join me on the Journey friends, it's good to have you along for the ride. Now it is time to get back to resorting it up in a paradise because trading has went that well.

www.ingramcontent.com/pod-product-compliance
Lightning Source LLC
Chambersburg PA
CBHW020601220526
45463CB00006B/2405